This book belongs to:
Use the nicknames you have for one another on the lines below!

&

Copyright © 2018 by Stacey M. Jailall

All rights reserved. This book or any portion thereof may not be reproduced or used in any manner whatsoever without the express written permission of the publisher except for the use of brief quotations in a book review.

Book Design By Stacey M. Jailall
of Think Branding
www.ThinkBrandingco.com

ISBN 978-0-578-42978-6

Independently Published

Thanks & Dedications

First & foremost, I'd like to give thanks as well as dedicate this entire book to the most special person in my life, **Mr. Joshua Walker**. Thank you for loving me the way you do. You are everything I've ever dreamed of & so much more. To say that I couldn't have written this book without you in my corner is a huge understatement! Not only do you constantly shower me with love, but you motivate me to be the best me that I can be every single day! You are the epitome of greatness and perfection in my eyes and I could not have ever imagined in a hundred years that I would ever meet someone who complements me the way you do. I could go on & on for days, but I'll simply sum it up with these three words: *I love you!*

Secondly, I'd like to thank my parents! Thank you for all that you do for me and all that you've ever sacrificed for me. I love you both so very much and although I may not show it all the time, you mean the world to me!

Thirdly, I'd like to give a huge shoutout to anyone who has ever supported me in any way, shape, or form. You all motivate me, encourage me, and help me to believe that I'm capable of achieving anything & everything that I put my mind to. I thank you all from the bottom of my heart for all of your kind words, donations, likes, purchases, shares, & more!

Last, but definitely not least, thank you God. I'm far from religious, but one thing I do know is that God has always been on my side and continues to prove that to me with the blessings I receive each & every day.

Congrats!

You've made it past all of my mushy-gushy thank you's! Now, I'll fill you in on a few things I'd like you to know before you dive into the book!

What should you expect to get out of this workbook?

This workbook serves as a guide to help you and your partner gain a new understanding of yourselves & your relationship! Think of this as getting to know your partner all over again!

How will I know if "Just You & I" is the workbook for me?

If you've been in any of the following situations with your partner, this book is for you:

- You have been bickering with or getting irritated with your partner over small occurances and you don't understand the root cause
- You feel like your partner isn't putting in the same effort that they did in the beginning
- You and your partner have lost that spark that you once had and are looking for ways to get it back
- When things are good, they're great, but really horrible when things get shaky
- You & your partner are doing just fine, but you're all about growth, so why not?
- You and your partner are happily in love and don't need any external help!

If you haven't noticed yet, if you're in a relationship, this book is for you!

Why Did I create this workbook ?

I created this workbook to promote improved communication between romantic partners; particularly those striving for long-term commitment. This workbook serves as a guide to learning how to communicate effectively with your partner at your own pace and in your own way. Inside you'll find a series of questions and activities that will help both you of you identify where you are as individuals as well as where you're at within your relationship. I believe that no matter what the status of the relationship is, broken or not, there will always be room for growth and improvement! Often times there are relationships that have ended prematurely due to a lack of proper communication. My goal is to end the cycle of prematurely broken relationships; I want to guide couples through the process of understanding and speaking about their past traumas as well as figuring out what their next steps are to either resolving or forgiving those incidents. My goal isn't to tell you how or what to do within your relationship, I simply want to help you lay out the facts so that you may implement solutions of your own. Lastly, I want this book to serve as a safe haven for you and your partner. Even if there are times where you aren't willing to hear your partner out, turn to this book to help you with getting used to creating a safe space for allowing your partner to speak to you about their feelings and emotions *without judgement or bias*. Last thing for real this time, don't worry about having enough space for your responses, talk out your answers and only jot down the main points to reference back to in the future, my goal is to have you both engaging in deep conversations the entire time!

My own relationship has had its own trials and tribulations, but because Joshua and I have implement this system of speaking and caring for our relationship the way we would with our health and careers, we've been able to build a more than solid foundation for our relationship to stand on whenever things get a little shaky!

Within this workbook, you will find the following topics:

Who am I

It's so important to be introspective before focusing on what's going on outside of yourself. You must first understand that both self-evaluation and self awareness play a huge role in how you see the world and treat others, so it's a must that this section comes first.

Before We Met

This section covers past relationships. Without closure from the past, there leaves room for disaster within your current relationship; to avoid this, you both must address the past with open minds and be willing to let go of or forgive anything that has put a strain on your lives or your relationship.

The Beginning of Us

Relive the moments that made you laugh, cry, or both. This is where you'll talk about the beginning of your current relationship! Here, you'll understand what drew you toward your partner, what made you stay, and you'll even deal with any situations between the two of you that may need closure.

Being Us

Relationships change over time and what you are dealing with in the present and how you handle situations in this stage is extremely vital to your future together. Do you feel that everything is fine and dandy or could the relationship use some work? Could your partner be a little more romantic or a little less argumentative? Let it all out in this section to help create a system of effective solutions for the future!

What Our Future Holds

In this section, you'll speak about what the future holds for the two of you and how you're going to reach each of the goals you have planned! Remember to tie each goal to a specific date or time period to hold yourselves accountable!

Loving You Better

This entire workbook is focused on communicating with your partner more effectively, but this section just breaks it down a bit further. Here, both you and your partner will learn how to perfect the art of loving one another.

Weekly Check-ins

Last, but certainly not least, we have our weekly check-in section. This is where you'll learn how to create a system of communicating with your partner more frequently so that your relationship is constantly growing and thriving!

This book includes:
- Some of my personal stories
- Tons of insightful questions both you and your partner must ask yourselves and one another
- Fun dates to do with your partner at the end of each section

The Rules of "Just you & I":

Below are some of the rules you must follow in order to make the most out of this book:

1. Be open minded!
Being open minded allows for both you and your partner to trust one another and easily open up without fear of being judged.

2. Be honest with yourself & your partner!
If you aren't honest, I promise that you will NOT gain anything from this book. I will warn you now, there are some pretty uncomfortable questions that you must answer, so be prepared for those! Try to think of this book as a *reset button*. This is meant to be your chance to move forward with 100% honesty about all of your feelings, but remember to always be respectful!

3. Be realistic and open to change!
Be open to growing and changing for the better. Keep your morals and values in mind, but if you have any negative habits or traits that you've been meaning to let go of, please do so!

4. Have conversations with your partner!
I really can't stress this enough! Don't just answer the questions, have conversations with each other and only jot down main points!

5. No skipping ahead
Please complete this entire workbook in order!

6. No Rushing
This book should take about 3 months to complete if you are truly dedicating the time to answer each question thoroughly.

Speak softly & listen loudly.

-Stacey Jailall

Section 1

Who am I

Section 1: Who am I

In this first section, both of you will be doing some crucial self-evaluation! The human experience is lifelong, so we must continue to learn and grow each and every day. I'm a firm believer in understanding who you are outside of your relationship before speaking about any issues that it may or may not have; that's why this section is first! The goal of this portion of the book is to help you evaluate where you are right now, where you came from, & where you want to be. Once you figure that out, you'll be able to create a roadmap with the steps you'll need to take in order to accomplish your goals! I wanted to put this book out as an ebook as well at one point, but I stopped myself from doing so because there is something so powerful about writing down your deepest thoughts and emotions in order to reflect on who you are as a person. It's almost like a mirror to your soul. It helps you easily plan out your short term and long term goals and also puts the battery in your back to *make them happen!* You are also able to hold yourself accountable for any goals that you haven't reached or even applaud yourself for all of the things that you are now able to check off your list! Once you're finished with this section, be sure to come back to it and reevaluate yourself at least every 3 months to see how far you've come!

In this section, you will:

- Further understand yourself (mind, body, & spirit)
- Embrace & love yourself more
- Create a list of standards as well as live up to those standards yourself
- Reflect on current relationships with friends and family
- Learn about how positive events in the past or even trauma has shaped you into who you are today
- Evaluate your next steps

Self Evaluation

In this first activity, you both will check off any traits that describe your personalities! Remember to be honest with your answers & while you're checking things off, discuss why you feel each trait fits your personality! Use half-checks for things that only somewhat apply. Throughout the book, feel free to take turns going first! Just remember to indicate who is answering by jotting down your initials in the boxes!

I am...

	initials go here	initials go here
Intelligent	☐	☐
Wise	☐	☐
Joyful	☐	☐
Willing to grow	☐	☐
Complacent	☐	☐
Optimistic	☐	☐
Pessimistic	☐	☐
Realistic	☐	☐
Confident	☐	☐
Cocky	☐	☐
Self Conscious	☐	☐
Focused	☐	☐
Often distracted	☐	☐
Logical	☐	☐
Creative	☐	☐
Judgemental	☐	☐
Open minded	☐	☐
Caring	☐	☐

I am... ☐ ☐

Aggressive	☐	☐
Passive Aggressive	☐	☐
Petty	☐	☐
Mature	☐	☐
Immature	☐	☐
Understanding	☐	☐
Free spirited	☐	☐
Conservative	☐	☐
Short tempered	☐	☐
Unbothered	☐	☐
Irrational	☐	☐
Rational	☐	☐
Energetic/Hyper	☐	☐
Laid back	☐	☐
Selfish	☐	☐
Selfless	☐	☐
Disciplined	☐	☐
Indisciplined	☐	☐
Well mannered	☐	☐
Rude	☐	☐
Depressed	☐	☐
Calm	☐	☐
Anxious	☐	☐
Paranoid	☐	☐

I am...

	☐	☐
Confrontational	☐	☐
Nonconfrontational	☐	☐
Insecure	☐	☐
Secure	☐	☐
Couragous	☐	☐
Self absorbed	☐	☐
Passionate	☐	☐
Passive	☐	☐

Some words that weren't listed that describe me are:

☐ _____

_____

_____

☐ _____

_____

_____

A word from Stace:

Be as honest as possible about the traits that make you who you are, even the bad stuff. There are lots of things I don't like about myself including my short temper or lack of discipline sometimes, but admitting that those are my faults helps me understand how I can fix them as well as what my goals should be!

What are some of the personality traits (listed or not) that I love about myself?

☐ _____
  _____
  _____

☐ _____
  _____
  _____

What are some of the personality traits (listed or not) that I dislike about myself?

☐ _____
  _____
  _____

☐ _____
  _____
  _____

What steps can I take to change the traits that I dislike about myself?

☐   ☐

What are some of the physical attributes that I love about myself?

☐ _____
   _____
   _____

☐ _____
   _____
   _____

What are some of the physical attributes that I dislike about myself?

☐ _____
   _____
   _____

☐ _____
   _____
   _____

What steps can I take to either change or embrace the things I dislike about my physical appearance?

☐   ☐

Why do I want to change or embrace the physical attributes that I dislike about myself?

☐ _____
_____

☐ _____
_____

Am I happy with my current physical health (Circle yes or no)? Write why or why not on the lines provided.

☐ **yes / no** _____
_____

☐ **yes / no** _____
_____

What are the steps that I can take to maintain or improve my physical health?

☐ _____
_____

☐ _____
_____

A word from Stace:

When I mentioned the word "change" on one of the the previous questions, I didn't at all mean that you need to go out and get surgery on the parts of you that you feel are subpar! That is why I also mentioned the word "embrace". For me, I've always had an issue with my weight. I have a condition called PCOS that actually makes me gain weight like crazy (along with a bunch of other symptoms) if I don't stay away from certain foods (carbs in particular, yes, fruits included!) I've even struggled with an eating disorder multiple times because of the effects of it, but these days I'm slowly learning to embrace what God gave me. Now, I take small steps each and every day to change how I eat. I've become more consistent with working out and I always keep my end goals in mind to keep me grounded! If you have certain physical features that you aren't too fond of, learn to love them. They make you who you are! If you'd like to lose weight, gain weight, or tighten up, do that! But first, be honest with yourself, be honest about what your goals are, and be honest with WHY they are your goals. Do you want to lose weight to be healthy, or do you just want to look good? There isn't anything wrong with either answer. Just understand your why & absolutely nothing can stop you!

What is the current state of my mental health & why?

More words from Stace:

Mental health is nothing to play with. For some reason, there is a negative stigma toward seeking professional help, but in all honesty, it's so theraputic and empowering. I started going to therapy in October of 2018 for anxiety and depression. I can honestly say that since then, I haven't been depressed at all and it's helped lower my anxiety like crazy! There was a point where I would miss out on events because I was so scared of going out and meeting new people. I've even cried right before heading out to an event that my own friends invited me to! It was no joke, but I knew that I wanted to make some changes and what I needed was some external help.

Joshua and I have always talked about everything; before therapy, he was my therapist, he still is, but it's nice to have an unbiased professional view about everything I'm going through - even things I go through with him. Therapy helps me see things a bit clearer and so far it's going great. My therapist happens to be someone I've grown to look up to. She's so supportive and motherly and has truly helped boost my confidence.

I highly recommend therapy as a form of self care, even if things are going seemingly well; you should always think about *preventative measures*.

What are some steps I could take *-or-* What steps am I currently taking to improve my mental health?

☐ _____
  _____

☐ _____
  _____

What are my spiritual or religious views?

☐   ☐

♥

Do I understand who I am as a person? How so?

☐   **yes / no** _____
_____

☐   **yes / no** _____
_____

A word from Stace:
We wake up everyday with a new opportunity to truly understand ourselves. It's okay to not fully understand who you are at the moment. I personally don't even fully get myself sometimes, but that's the beauty of life! Learn every day, have faith, & just try your best to be greater than you were yesterday!

When I was younger, where did I see myself at this age? (Career, financial, relationship status, kids, etc.)

What I envisioned (previous question) compared to where I am now...

☐   ☐

Am I happy with where I am today? Why am I happy ?

Where do I see myself in 5 years?

A word from Stace:

Life takes a lot of unexpected turns, sometimes it may seem like it's for the worst, but it's always for the best. I don't think anything happens by accident. I feel that everything we go through has a purpose, whether it is to teach us, guide us to our next destination, or block us from something that wasn't meant for us, everything happens for a reason.

When I was younger, I imagined that I would be a pediatrician by the age of 22 (How? Who knows!) I wanted to find the love of my life at 20, buy a house at 22, get married at 25, have kids at 28, and live happily ever after! I had this whole life planned out for myself by the age of 11. There's absolutely nothing wrong with what my dreams were, and I'm sure if my dreams didn't change, I would've made them happen, but they changed and I'm happy to say that I made adjustments! Today, I'm 26, I have my own branding company (shameless plug: www.thinkbrandingco.com), a surprise travel company with my boyfriend (www.projectgetawaytrip.com), & I also help him in any way that I can with his nonprofit (www.amger.org), oh yeah, I'm also the proud author of this workbook, so I guess you could say I'm beyond happy with all of my career choices! As far as my relationship goes, I met Joshua aka the love of my life at 23, we started dating at 24, and in the near future, we'll get married, buy our house, have our little munchkins, and continue to live happily ever after. Although I'm not exactly where I expected to be when I was 11, I know that I'm right where I need to be for now and I'm loving every moment of my journey. I hope that you both appreciate where you are in life and just continue to strive to be the best at whatever you decide to do!

How do I feel about my career/job?

☐ _____
　_____
_____

☐ _____
　_____
_____

What are the next steps to furthering or maintaining my career?

☐　　　　　☐

What are some of my hobbies? How often do I make time for them?

☐ _____
　_____
_____

☐ _____
　_____
_____

How do I handle conflict with my family and friends?

☐ _____
_____

☐ _____
_____

How do I handle conflicts at work?

☐ _____
_____

☐ _____
_____

What is my current relationship with my family? Where would I like it to be in the future?

☐ _____
_____
_____
_____

☐ _____
_____
_____
_____

What is my current relationship with my friends?

☐ _____
  _____
  _____

☐ _____
  _____
  _____

Where would I like my relationship with my friends to be in the future?

☐ _____
  _____

☐ _____
  _____

What was my upbringing like? (Be as specific and open as possible)

☐   ☐

What are some experiences that made me who I am?

☐ _____
_____
_____

☐ _____
_____
_____

Did I go through any traumatic experiences growing up? How did they affect me?

☐ _____
_____
_____
_____

☐ _____
_____
_____
_____

Have I healed from this trauma? Do I have a plan to begin my healing process? What is my plan?

☐ _____
_____

☐ _____
_____

Do I often, if ever, let pride control my feelings and emotions? Why or why not & how can I work on this?

Do I have any insecurities? (ex: Comparing myself to others) Be as honest with yourself as possible!

What standards do I have for romantic relationships? Do I live up to these standards myself?

yes / no   yes / no

What can I do to start living up to my own standards? (If no to last question) How can I maintain living up to my standards (If yes)?

☐ _____
_____
_____

☐ _____
_____
_____

A word from Stace:

There are a few things I'd like to comment on regarding that section:

1. **Standards:** They're a great tool to have to protect ourselves from heartaches or disappointments, but sometimes we forget to live up to our own standards or don't even realize that we aren't living up to them. Love should absolutely be unconditional, but realistically, like-mindedness is what keeps people together whether it be romantically or platonically. If we want extraordinary people in our lives, we must be extraordinary people ourselves.

2. **Trauma & the past:** Most of us have gone through traumatic experiences in life; whether they're big or small, they've happened. What we need to do is acknowledge that the trauma we've encountered has either changed or impacted us in some way and learn to grow from what we've experienced. Having been hurt in the past is no excuse to hurt people. Learn from the past and never allow it to dictate your future!

Now that you've completed this section, you have a clear idea of all of the changes that you'd like to make as well as all of the things you're happy with! Below, list the first 3 goals you want to focus on accomplishing this week!

Remember to think: mind, body, & spirit!

Self Evaluation Goals!

Section Recap: How do I feel?

Below, write a brief recap of how you felt while completing this section.

☐ _____
_____
_____
_____

☐ _____
_____
_____
_____

A word from Stace:

Please don't let your self evaluation end here! I recommend that you frequently check in on yourselves using this guide to ensure that you are both knocking out the goals that you've set for yourself! Don't forget to also serve as "accountability partners" for one another to keep each other on the right track! Continuous self evaluation has helped me by providing me with insight on myself, this allows me to communicate better with my partner. By being as honest as possible about all of my insecurities and traumas, I'm able to understand what I do and don't want in my life so that I can make my standards clear to him and vice versa. I hope that this section has given you more of a perspective on who you are, too!

Now, onto your first activity together!

Date Roulette!

You've made it through the first section of the book! It's time to relax a little & enjoy one anothers company! So sit back, relax, & read the rules of Date Roulette to see what your first activity holds!

So what exactly is Date Roulette?

Date roulette is exactly what it sounds like. Below, you and your partner will both write down **two numbers each** between 1 - 10 (you can choose a number more than once; ex: 4, 4, 4, 6). Once they're all chosen, you'll go on the dates with the corresponding numbers on the next page! Sounds fun? Okay, let's do this!

Once you've chosen your numbers, head to the next page & read off the numbers from left to right (one number per column) to see where you're going on your day out with your sweety! Jot down where you're going on the lines below to remember your first "Just you & I" date! Feel free to come back & play as many times as you want!

_____
_____
_____
_____

# Date

Fun Activities!

1. Sky Zone
2. Bike Ride
3. Pottery Class
4. Movie Date
5. Short Hike
6. Make Chocolate at a chocolate factory!
7. Museum
8. Ice Skating
9. Laser Tag & Arcade
10. Pop-up Event (An event or shop that is only in town for a limited time)

1. Paint & Sip
2. Comedy Show
3. Escape Room
4. Roller Skating
5. Bowling
6. Open Mic Event
7. (Off) Broadway show
8. Volunteer together
9. Game Cafe
10. Take a drive or walk to a nice view & enjoy the sunset

Once you've figured out what your plans are, feel free to choose whatever day you'd like to have your date as well as the times that you'd like to do each activity!

Roulette

Good Eats!

1. Sushi
2. Wings
3. Mexican Food
4. Hamburgers & Shakes
5. Pizza
6. Gourmet Salad
7. Chinese Food
8. Vegan Only Spot
9. Soup & Sammiches!
10. Bakery/Cafe (Treats!)

1. Stay at home & cook
2. Steakhouse
3. Thai Food
4. Southern Spot
5. Italian Restaurant
6. Churrascaria (Order the Rodizio)
7. American Restaurant
8. Cook your own food styled restaurant (The Melting Pot)
9. Seafood
10. Hibachi

Remember to take lots of pictures! & Don't forget to hashtag **#justyouandibook** for a chance to be featured on my instagram page @stacey_jayyy!

Section 2

Before
We Met

Section 2: Before We Met

This next step will be a little uncomfortable, but it's just as necessary as the rest of the book. Here, you'll express to your partner the good, the bad, and the ugly about your past relationships and experiences with previous significant others. Please be as honest as possible. Understanding what your partner felt within his or her past relationships will benefit your current relationship in so many ways. You know what they say "those who cannot learn from history are doomed to repeat it." This is why I like to be upfront and talk about everything with Joshua! I want to know what he liked and what he absolutely despised so that I can use it to make our relationship better and stronger. You should also keep in mind that your partner obviously had good moments within their previous relationships - they were with those people for a reason. Take the past experiences that your partner shares with you and use them to build your relationship up rather than use what they share with you against them the future. **Remember**, this is a safe space!

In this section, you will:

- Recognize what worked and what didn't work within your last relationship
- Understand your toxic traits as well as your ex's within the previous relationship you had with them
- Understand whether or not your ex left you with any insecurities
- Evaluate whether or not you are completely over past situations and traumas from previous relationships

Before We Met

Have I spoken to my partner about my past relationships? Why or why not?

☐ **yes / no** _____
_____
_____
_____

☐ **yes / no** _____
_____
_____
_____

Beyond physical features, what attracted me to my last partner? (Think personality traits!)
This tracks where you have grown or what you have stayed consistent with when looking for a partner.

☐ _____
_____

☐ _____
_____

Have I brought over any insecurities or baggage from past relationships? Yes or No? If yes, what are they?

☐ yes / no _____
_____
_____

☐ yes / no _____
_____
_____

Am I still friends with any of my exes? If so, how does my partner feel about it?

☐ yes / no _____
_____
_____

☐ yes / no _____
_____
_____

Am I completely over the past (trauma, pain, etc.)? Yes or no? Explain how you know this.

☐ _____
_____
_____

☐ _____
_____
_____

What did I like about my last relationship?

☐ _____
_____
_____

☐ _____
_____
_____

What did I dislike about my last relationship?

☐ _____
_____
_____

☐ _____
_____
_____

Why did my last relationship end?

☐ _____
_____

☐ _____
_____

A word from Stace:

Speaking about the past shouldn't be difficult, I understand that sometimes it might be, but that's only because we make it that way. Joshua and I welcome each others stories of the past all the time, but there was a point a little over a year ago that he brought it to my attention that I was making petty remarks about one of his past relationships. It wasn't until he pointed it out to me that I even noticed I was doing it. He even calmly mentioned that she was the same way sometimes and it was something that used to bother him in the past. It annoyed me to hear that we had any similar qualities, but I was happy that he was honest and I was able to grow from that situation. Moral of the story: We all make mistakes, sometimes we don't even realize it, but the key is learning from them! *Sometimes* we're the reason our partner doesn't want to open up or doesn't feel like being completely honest about a situation (sometimes, not always, so don't blame yourself if they're just straight up hiding things from you without reason). Sharing stories about my past with Joshua makes me feel like I'm truly speaking to my best friend; someone who wants to hear about what I've been through to learn more about who I am rather than judge me for what I've done or been through, I absolutely love it! Being honest with someone is so easy when they make you feel comfortable. With previous partners, I felt as though I was in a relationship where I couldn't talk about my past. My partner would constantly make me feel judged, so I would often keep things to myself. It's hard to be with someone when you can't be yourself. I say all of this to say that we should always be open to learning about our partners past. If you feel like you haven't been trying your best to learn or vice versa, make a note of whenever you say something that may make your partner feel a type of way, sincerely apologize for it, & then grow from it!

What were the toxic traits my partner had in my last relationship?

☐ _____
_____

☐ _____
_____

What were the toxic traits I had in my last relationship?

☐ _____
_____

☐ _____
_____

What were some complaints that my previous partner had about me?

☐ _____
_____
_____

☐ _____
_____
_____

How did my last partner make me feel within our relationship? (Circle all that apply in your own sections)

Insecure	Worthy	Insecure	Worthy
Secure	Unworthy	Secure	Unworthy
Happy	Anxious	Happy	Anxious
Sad	Calm	Sad	Calm
Jealous	Motivated	Jealous	Motivated
Comfortable	Unmotivated	Comfortable	Unmotivated

What are some things that I learned from past relationships that shaped me into the person I am today?

_____
_____
_____
_____

_____
_____
_____
_____

Did I go through any traumatic experiences in the past? (Been cheated on, physical/mental abuse, etc.)

_____
_____
_____

_____
_____
_____

A word from Stace:

This section was a little heavy! Sorry about that, but these conversations are absolutely necessary for growth! A few things that I wanted to recap were toxic traits and trauma! Understanding the toxic traits that we had in past relationships can help us distinguish whether or not we still carry some of those traits with us today. Once we realize that we might still have these toxic traits, we need to address them with a plan of how we're going to fix them - remember, these are the things that could potentially make or break our relationships now!

As for trauma, I know I addressed this in one of the previous sections, but it must be reiterated that although we've all dealt with some form of trauma in our lives, it gives us no right to treat others with anything less than the utmost respect. We may have been hurt in the past by family, friends, or partners, but what we must do is forgive the past. It happened, it's over, you survived, and now you're stronger. Seek therapy for situations that you feel you haven't completely healed from and be open and honest with your partner about anything that may potentially impact your relationship.

Remember: Communication is key!

Section Recap: How do I feel?

Is there any trauma you need to overcome? How will you begin your healing?
If you do not need healing, briefly describe how you both felt completing this section.

☐ _____
_____
_____
_____
_____
_____
_____
_____

☐ _____
_____
_____
_____
_____
_____
_____
_____

Don't overlook the lessons that pain can teach you by crying over it more than once.

-Stacey Jailall

Our Indoor Date Night

Yay! We're finally another section down, so you know what that means... It's time to pat yourselves on the back & take some time to appreciate one another with the next date! This one is simple & can be done from the comfort of your own home! Just follow the instructions below to begin your date!

❤ **Make a Playlist of 30 or more of your favorite songs!**

Choose songs that came out when you first got together, songs that make you think of your bae, -or- songs that you've dedicated to one another!

❤ **Cook the following meal together!**
(Look up your fav recipies for the following & Listen to your playlist while cooking!)

Appetizer: Tomato Mozzarella Salad
Main Dish: Homemade copycat Jack Daniels Sauce (recipe on next page) Steak (or your choice of meat or meat substitute)
Sides: Garlic mashed potatoes and broccoli
Dessert: Chocolate Fudge Brownies & Ice Cream or substitute with your favorite treat!

❤ **End the night off with a movie!**
Watch one or more of the movies listed on the next page to end off your perfect date! If your movie has more than one part, you must watch all of them! (See list of movies after Jack Daniels recipe!)

Homemade copycat Jack Daniels Sauce!

1 head garlic
1 tablespoon olive oil
1 1/3 cups dark brown sugar
1 cup pineapple juice
2/3 cup water
1/4 cup teriyaki sauce
1 tablespoon soy sauce
3 tablespoons lemon juice
3 tablespoons minced white onion
1 tablespoon bourbon whiskey
1 tablespoon crushed pineapple
1/4 teaspoon cayenne pepper

How to prepare it

Preheat oven to 325 degrees F (165 degrees C).
Cut about 1/2-inch from the top of the garlic head. Trim the roots so the garlic sits flat. Remove some of the outer layers of papery skin from the garlic, leaving enough so that the cloves stay together. Put garlic into a small casserole dish or baking dish, drizzle olive oil over it, and cover with a lid or aluminum foil. Roast garlic in preheated oven until the cloves are soft, about 1 hour.
Stir brown sugar, pineapple juice, water, teriyaki sauce, and soy sauce together in a saucepan and bring to a boil; reduce heat to low and keep at simmer.
Squeeze sides of the garlic until the pasty roasted garlic emerges. Measure 2 teaspoons roasted garlic into the saucepan and incorporate into the sauce with a whisk. Reserve remaining roasted garlic for another use.
Stir lemon juice, white onion, bourbon whiskey, pineapple, and cayenne pepper into the sauce; bring to a simmer and cook until the volume of the liquid reduces by half and is thick and syrup-like, 40 to 50 minutes.

Recipe via: www.allrecipes.com

Movie List!

Choose a movie from the list below! These are some of my favorites! Remember, if your movie has more than one part, you must watch all of them!

- Wreck it Ralph
- Back to the Future 1, 2, & 3
- The Sixth Sense
- Predestination
- Momento
- Before I Go to Sleep
- Shutter Island
- Inception
- Horrible Bosses 1 & 2
- We're the Millers
- Game Night
- Inside Out
- Meet the Robinsons
- Crash
- Searching
- Thurgood
- Avengers
- The Other Woman
- Click
- The Shawshank Redemption
- The Uninvited
- Molly's Game

Remember to take lots of pictures! & Don't forget to hashtag **#justyouandibook** for a chance to be featured on my instagram page @stacey_jayyy!

Section 3

The Beginning of Us

Section 3: The Beginning of Us

The beginning of our relationships are usually all rainbows and butterflies, some may even refer to this stage as "the honeymoon phase". My question is, why can't the honeymoon phase last forever? Why did we become comfortable with the idea that the initial spark from our relationships are supposed to fade away? I think it's important to remember what it was that grabbed our partners attention from the beginning and actively pursue them using the same actions long after you've been together. Both you and your partner will feel immensely loved and appreciated if the "little things" you did in the beginning were to become a normal routine once again! Throughout this section, you will also be given the opportunity to speak about any issues that have been lingering in the shadows of your relationship, these are the things that you haven't been able to get full closure on. It's important that these issues are settled before moving forward. Resentment is one of the biggest killers of all relationships!

In this section, you will:

- Identify what attracted you to your partner
- Get the proper closure for any situations that may need it (ex: distrust in the past, something hurtful one of you has said or done, etc.)
- Remind yourselves to work for the relationship
- Be open to talking about any and all feelings that you have toward one another (good or bad)
- Be open to all criticism, hold yourself accountable for any situations that require you to do so

Tip: When reading the questions, anything with a (*) next to it requires that you and your partner ask the question to one another instead of asking yourselves.

The Beginning of Us

How did we meet? (Tell your story from each one of your perspectives)

☐ _____
_____
_____
_____
_____
_____

☐ _____
_____
_____
_____
_____
_____

This is what initially attracted me to you (looks, aura, personality, scent, etc.)

☐ _____
_____

☐ _____
_____

This is what kept me interested in you...

☐ _____
_____
_____

☐ _____
_____
_____

*** What/when was the moment you realized you were falling for me?**

☐ _____
_____
_____

☐ _____
_____
_____

*** What made me stand out from everyone else?**
Cue the waterworks!

☐ _____
_____
_____

☐ _____
_____
_____

When did our "honeymoon phase" end & how did I realize it was over?

☐ _____
_____
_____
_____
_____
_____

☐ _____
_____
_____
_____
_____
_____

Is there anything that bothered me in the past that I never brought up? If so, explain.

☐ _____
_____
_____

☐ _____
_____
_____

When was our first argument? What was it about and how did we resolve it? (Write from your own perspectives)

☐ _____
_____
_____
_____
_____

☐ _____
_____
_____
_____
_____

Proceed with caution:
Does my partner know about my previous sexual partners? Why or why not?

Every relationship is different, it's not necessary to know your partners exact number, but this definitely helps measure how open you are with one another.

☐ _____
_____
_____
_____

☐ _____
_____
_____

* Have I done anything that you've needed to forgive me for in the past? How did that make you feel?

☐ _____
  _____
  _____

☐ _____
  _____
  _____

Have there been any infidelities within our relationship? If so, am I completely over them?

☐ _____
  _____
  _____

☐ _____
  _____
  _____

What are my absolute deal breakers?

☐ _____
  _____
  _____

☐ _____
  _____
  _____

Section Recap: How do I feel?

Briefly recap how you felt speaking about the beginning of your relationship.

☐ _____
_____
_____
_____
_____
_____
_____
_____
_____

☐ _____
_____
_____
_____
_____
_____
_____
_____

The honeymoon phase of your relationship never has to end.

-Stacey Jailall

Strolling Down Memory Lane

You're killing it! Only a few more sections left, but before you worry about that, it's time for an activity!

What you'll need:

- Mason Jar
- Scissors (2 pairs)
- Colored Construction Paper
- Pens or markers (2)

Instructions:

You both will be strolling down memory lane with this activity! First cut pieces of construction paper and use them to write down your best memories (25 small sheets each)! Once you've written all of your memories down, read them to one another, talk about them, relive the moment, & then toss them in the mason jar! Set a reminder to read these memories in 6 months and save any extra paper cutouts to add some new memories when you open it back up again! Use some of the examples below to get you started on your memory collection!

- Our First Kiss:
  Where & when was it?
  Who made the first move & how did it happen?

- Our First Date:
  Where & when did we go?
  How did it go & were you nervous?

- Our Favorite Adventure:
  Where did we go?
  What did we do & why was it our fav.?

- The first time we said I love you:
  Who said it first?
  Did the person who said it first get an "I love you" back?

Section 4

Being Us

Section 4: Being Us

We've gotten through the beginning of your relationship, now it's time to take a look at the current state of it! How does your partner make you feel today, how do you feel about your partner today, these are just a few questions you'll be asking yourself in this section! We'll be taking a look at all of the things that make you and your partner *you*! The goal of the questions you're about to embark on are to lay out all of the facts of your relationship and help you come up with a roadmap on how to solve any issues that may need resolving. If your relationship doesn't need any of that, then use what you'll learn in this section to reiterate what you're already doing and continue to be the most wonderful partner there is! Again, both of you must continue to be openminded and willing to accept criticism. Although you will both be dishing out critiques, make sure that you are both being realistic & respectful with what you are asking of your partner! Take baby steps to move forward if need be, but always keep one thing in mind: **"how can I grow from this"**?

In this section, you will:

- Acknowledge how you both have either evolved as a couple or stayed stagnant
- Create a roadmap of how you're going to resolve any issues that you're currently facing
- Be honest about the current state of your relationship in order to move forward with a clean slate
- Learn new ways to love your partner!

Tip: When reading the questions, anything with a (*) next to it requires that you and your partner both ask the question to one another instead of asking yourselves.

Being Us

What are the things that I love the most about you?

☐ _____
  _____
  _____

☐ _____
  _____
  _____

* Make a list of all of the ways I make you feel loved

☐   ☐

Has anything changed in regards to what attracted me to you?

☐ _____
  _____

  _____

☐ _____
  _____

  _____

Do I trust you? Why or why not?

☐ _____
  _____

  _____

☐ _____
  _____

  _____

Do I feel like I can be completely honest with you? Why or why not?

☐ _____
  _____

  _____

☐ _____
  _____

  _____

* Do you feel that I give you constructive criticism or am I too critical or judgemental of you? How so?

I feel like you respect me. True or false? Why or why not?

True / False

True / False

Do we get into arguments or disagreements? (How often?)

☐ _____

☐ _____

What are our arguments/disagreements about?

☐ _____

☐ _____

What are some of my pet peeves when it comes to you?

☐ _____

☐ _____

* What are some things you dislike about me?

☐ _____
_____
_____

☐ _____
_____
_____

* What are some things that I do for you that you appreciate?

☐ _____
_____
_____

☐ _____
_____
_____

What is my current relationship with your family and friends?

☐ _____
_____

☐ _____
_____

Are we comfortable with speaking about finances with one another? Why or why not?

☐ _____
  _____

☐ _____
  _____

Do I feel like you are supportive of my goals? How so?

☐ _____
  _____
  _____
  _____

☐ _____
  _____
  _____
  _____

What are some of the ways that you motivate me?

☐ _____
  _____
  _____
  _____

☐ _____
  _____
  _____
  _____

* **What are some additional ways that you feel I can help you achieve your goals?**

☐ _____
_____
_____

☐ _____
_____
_____

* **What do you feel that I can do to improve myself?**

☐ _____
_____
_____

☐ _____
_____
_____

* **Do you feel that I compliment you enough? What are some of the nice things I say to you?**

☐ _____
_____

☐ _____
_____

A word from Stace:

Hey there, how's it going so far? At this point, you've either learned or relearned a bunch of new things about your partner that can help you to better your relationship with one another! There's still way more to go, but I just wanted to quickly remind you that it's very easy to simply sit down & have a conversation about what needs to be done in order to move forward successfully, the hard part is executing and following through with making changes! When Josh and I first began doing meetings like this, we actually thought it was going to be a one time thing. We read a book by Leonardo Cavalli titled "24 and Divorced" (definitely a recommended read) and at the end, there were 20 questions for couples to ask one another before they considered getting married. We read this book when we were still in our "honeymoon phase", so it came to us at just the right moment. Up until that point everything seemed to be going exceptionally well, we were #goals in our eyes just until we received our rude awakening. The book helped us realize that there were some hidden resentments that we had toward one another that we didn't even know existed until we sat down and answered the tough evaluation questions. We like to be very proactive, so after answering the questions, we came up with solutions for how to solve our issues, but we needed a way to track our progress. That's how our meetings were born, later on in the book I'll explain those in further detail and help you both set up meetings of your own! Our meetings were able to help us redefine the phrase "honeymoon phase" in so many ways! Sure, there are times when things aren't perfect, but we've created a safe haven to speak about the *toughest* things we go through with one another without fear of being judged or criticized for our feelings!

* Am I as romantic/spontaneous as you'd like me to be? How can I work on this?

☐ _____
_____
_____

☐ _____
_____
_____

* Are our morals aligned with one another? What makes you feel this way?

☐ _____
_____
_____

☐ _____
_____
_____

* Are there things that I do that you don't agree with?

☐ _____
_____

☐ _____
_____

* Has social media impacted our relationship in any way? Why or why not?

☐ _____
  _____

☐ _____
  _____

* What is it about me that makes you proud of me?

☐ _____
  _____
  _____
  _____

☐ _____
  _____
  _____
  _____

* List your favorite physical qualities about me!

☐   ☐

Does my partner know everything about my past (outside of past relationships)? Why or why not?

☐ _____
_____
_____

☐ _____
_____
_____

Am I happy with the current state of our relationship? Why or why not?

☐ _____
_____
_____

☐ _____
_____
_____

* Do I bring out the best in you? How so?

☐ _____
_____

☐ _____
_____

Are we spending too little or too much time together? (I feel this way because...)

☐ _____
_____
_____

☐ _____
_____
_____

How do other people view my partner? (Is he/she respected, loved, the life of the party, etc.)

☐ _____
_____
_____

☐ _____
_____
_____

* How do you feel about me sexually & how is our sex life?

☐ _____
_____

☐ _____
_____

Since we've been together, this is how I've changed for the better...

☐ _____
_____
_____

☐ _____
_____
_____

Since we've been together, these are the ways that I feel you've changed for the better...

☐ _____
_____
_____

☐ _____
_____
_____

These are the ways you make me happy...

☐ _____
_____

☐ _____
_____

Based on what we learned within this section, these are 3 ways that we can improve our relationship. (Write 3 each & feel free to write more if you need to!)

A word from Stace:

Congrats! You've completed the most difficult section of the book: The present! A lot of times, we're afraid to address the present because we feel that it might jeopardize our relationship. My advice is to go into every situation with a "fix it" mentality. Speak to your partner with respect and gentle tones. We're all adults, we don't need to yell at, curse at, or belittle one another. Handle the situation with open mindedness and the willingness to see things from your partners perspective. Remember proper communication is the only way to fix any issues you both are currently facing!

Section Recap: How do I feel?

Express how you felt speaking about the present of your relationship. Do you see differences from when you first got together?

☐ _____

_____
_____
_____
_____
_____
_____
_____
_____
_____

☐ _____

_____
_____
_____
_____
_____
_____
_____
_____
_____

Good relationships: Two people who love one another just the way they are. Great Relationships: Two people who love one another just the way they are, but continue to push each other to new limits so they can become the best versions of themselves.

-Stacey Jailall

We're having a game night!

As you may already know, relationships are more than just the two of you. They're made up of your "tribe", the group of people that you both love and care about!
Whether it be friends or family, we all have people that we love in our lives and any opportunity to get together with them should be jumped at! That's why, for this activity, you'll be hosting a **game night** & you're inviting your closest friends and family!

What you'll need!

- Food or Snacks
- **Soft drinks or Drinks Drinks (Adult beverages)**
- Games!
- Prizes (You can't go wrong with gag gifts!)
- Homemade Decorations (Optional)
- Plates & Utensils
- Napkins
- Music
- Your A-Game!

If you want, you can even have guests bring their own snacks and drinks & you can supply the rest, this makes the night more cost efficient for the two of you!

Night!

Recommended Games

- Cards Against Humanity
- Taboo
- Charades/Heads up
- Uno (Prepare to destroy the very friendships you love)
- Pictionary
- Jenga
- 5 Second Rule

Option 2: Game night, minus the planning!

Let's face it, as great as it sounds, maybe we don't have the time or resources just yet to host a game night. If your schedule is a little crazy, or funds are a little tight, or you'd like to skip the planning, but you still want to spend time with the coolest people you know, plan a game night at your nearest **game cafe**! Game cafe's are super fun, affordable, they have ready to order meals and drinks, and of course, all of the games you can imagine! **Enjoy!**

Don't forget to take lots of pictures! & Don't forget to hashtag **#justyouandibook** for a chance to be featured on my instagram page @stacey_jayyy!

Section 5

What Our Future Holds

Section 5: What Our Future Holds

The future is always a day away, but remember that what you are doing now will impact the overall outcome of your life. Although we are going to speak about the future in this short section, keep in mind all of the things you must do now in order to reach your combined goals. Remember that there is no dream too big to dream, you just need to make sure that you have the work ethic to *make it happen!* When speaking about the future of your relationship, you may need to do a lot of compromising. Why? Well, we all have our own preferences, just be sure to stand by your values instead of simply giving into your partners wants. When you are establishing things like where you want to live or what cars you want to buy, who will be cooking and cleaning, who will be handling the finances, or where you would like to travel to, ensure that it makes absolute sense and will work out in favor of your relationship. Don't let pride or gender roles stop you from doing things that aren't as masculine or feminine as you'd like! Last, but not least, understand your **why. Why** do you want to live in Wisconsin (that's the first place that popped into my head), Why do you want to give your kids time outs instead of spankings? Think about your why's to keep you both grounded and focused!

In this section, you will:

- Understand your individual goals for the future
- Understand your **Why's**
- Compromise on future goals
- Think about where you'd like the state of your relationship to be in the coming years

What Our Future Holds

Activity: Imagine the next 5 years with bae, what do you see for the two of you? In the matrix below, answer the following questions (answer separately then discuss)

	name:	name:
When will we get married? (The ideal year/month)		
We will have _ kids by then? (How many)		
We will live in (state/country) in this type of home:		
We'll drive: (this type of car)		
We'll have traveled to: (list all of your bucket list destinations)		
We'll have these pets:		

A word from Stace:

Sometimes, talking about the future can be frustrating, but as long as you're open to solutions, it's so worth it. For instance, Joshua and I have spoken about marriage before, we even planned out our whole wedding during a date night a few months ago, but we aren't engaged yet. We both understand that we want to be in a better place **financially** before embarking on the journey of marriage, plus we both understand our relationship and don't need to validate it with an expensive ring and huge wedding (not for now at least). Although I understood all of this when we initially spoke about it, I still made a remark during one of our weekly relationship meetings about how I wanted to be married, or at least engaged sometime soon. He asked me why and reminded me of all the things we previously spoke about. He assured me that he wants to get engaged just as badly as I do, but first we have to think responsibly and always consider our goals. When I thought about it, I was thankful that he brought me back to reality, I only wanted to put a rush on things because I was comparing myself to all of the people I saw around me getting engaged! When I thought about it more rationally, I realized that getting engaged wasn't a priority right now especially because it doesn't change anything but the title on our relationship. It's not the title that matters, it's the actual relationship! Although I know it'll happen one day, it doesn't have to be any time soon and I'm perfectly okay with that. When planning out your goals, keep in mind that they are YOUR goals and no one else's. Don't compare yourself to anyone else's timeline, you will accomplish everything that you need to when the time is right for **you**, just be patient.

Now, we're going to go a little more in depth!
Why or why don't I see myself marrying my partner?

☐ _____
_____

_____

☐ _____
_____

_____

Given our answers to where we want to live in the future, what location can we compromise on?

Think about this one long and hard: Who will be handling the finances/budget (*Me, You, Both of us*) & Why?

How are we going to raise our kids? (Type of discipline, Religion, Schooling, Activities/sports, etc.)

What holidays, traditions, & anniversaries will we celebrate?

In 5 years, this is where I would like my relationship with your family & friends to be:

☐ _____
_____
_____

☐ _____
_____
_____

Where do I see my career being in 5 years?

☐ _____
_____
_____

☐ _____
_____
_____

This is where I would like our finances to be in 5 years:

☐ _____
_____

☐ _____
_____

Based on all of our answers to the previous questions, are we currently doing all that we can to reach these goals? If not, what can we do to make these goals more reachable?

☐ _____
_____
_____

☐ _____
_____
_____

Are our goals aligned? Why do I feel this way?

☐ _____
_____
_____

☐ _____
_____
_____

Specify who will take care of each of these household chores (cooking, laundry, etc.) *Me, You, Both of us?*

☐ _____
_____
_____

☐ _____
_____
_____

Mind, Body, & Spirit

The mindset I'd like to have in 5 years:

☐ _____
_____
_____

☐ _____
_____
_____

The state of health I'd like to be in, in 5 years:

☐ _____
_____
_____

☐ _____
_____
_____

Where would I like my spirituality to be in 5 years?

☐ _____
_____
_____

☐ _____
_____
_____

One last question: How do we see the condition of our love in 5 years? (Still romantic, having fun together, etc.)

☐   ☐

Section Recap: How do I feel?

How did you feel talking about your future together?

☐ _____
_____
_____
_____
_____

☐ _____
_____
_____
_____
_____

Time to get creative!

Who said you were too old to color? For this activity, find some colored pencils & draw the ideal life you love birds would like to create for yourselves. (Ex: you both in front of your dream house with your kids, pets, cars, some friends, or whatever you'd like!)

Your future depends on all of the decisons you make now, so make 'em count!

- Stacey Jailall

Vision Board Night

I'm so excited that you're just zooming through this book! Hopefully you had some fun while coloring on the last page. Now that you've completed that section, it's time to make some vision boards! Vision boards are a fun and creative way to visualize where you'd like to be in the future. For this one, you'll be visualizing your life 10 years from now.

What you'll need:
- Magazines
- Scissors
- Glue
- Oaktag Paper

Instructions:
Head to the nearest grocery store and pick out some magazines that you think might have pictures and images of things you'll want to be or items you'd like to have in the future (ex: successful people, travel destinations, cars, powerful quotes, a family, a ring - the possibilities are endless)! Cut out all of the images and words that work for you. Once you've chosen your images, place them on the board. You both will be creating separate boards (if you live together, you may choose to combine one board & split it right down the middle). Feel free to add glitter or other colorful pieces to make your board(s) pop!

After Vision Board Completion:
Hang your board in a place where you'll see it all the time. This serves as a reminder for what you both want to accomplish and why you must continue to work hard!

Section 6

Loving You Better

Section 6: Loving You Better

This section is really short, but I promise it's super powerful! *Loving you better* is dedicated to understanding how your partner wants to be loved as well as how to notice the signs of what you could be doing better or differently within your relationship. Inspired by Gary Chapman's "The Five Love Languages", I feel like everyone has in mind that special love language that makes them tingle! It may not necessarily fall under the 5 love languages, but we all have a special way that we'd like to be loved. Don't get it? Let me explain: If you like being hugged constantly and all I do is buy you presents, then you may feel like I don't love you as much as I say I do. I may love you to with all my heart, but you can't see that because you're equating my love for you in the form of hugs and I haven't given you any of those in a while. We need to understand that everyone has their own preferences when it comes to how they'd like their love served to them & we must cater to this in a way that best suits their needs! Another way of being able to spot how to love your partner better is to notice how they love you! If you're constantly being showered with kisses, chances are your partner loves being kissed. One thing I don't recommend is that you wait and hope for your partner to love you how you want to be loved. A lot of times, we want the romantic things our partner does for us to be "genuine", so we don't mention our needs hoping that they'll just take a hint. This is actually so detrimental to relationships, you must help your partner understand what you want by talking to them about it in order to teach them how to love you better. I don't believe in psychics or mind readers, so help your partners or be prepared for disappointment.

In this section, you will:

- Understand how your partner wants to be loved
- Speak about where you feel appreciated and under appreciated
- Become the best partner you've ever been

Loving You Better

How do I show love to my partner?

☐ _____
_____

☐ _____
_____

What are some of the things that my partner does that makes me feel loved?

☐ _____
_____

☐ _____
_____

What are some things that I do for my partner that go unnoticed?

☐ _____
_____

☐ _____
_____

Do I show appreciation for my partner? How so?

☐ _____
   _____
   _____

☐ _____
   _____
   _____

Do I feel like my partner shows appreciation for me? How so?

☐ _____
   _____
   _____

☐ _____
   _____
   _____

What could my partner do to make me feel more loved?

☐   ☐

How do I currently communicate my anger to my partner?

☐ _____
  _____

☐ _____
  _____

What can I do to improve how I express anger toward my partner?

☐ _____
  _____

☐ _____
  _____

Relationships revolve around compromise, is there anything we can't compromise on?

☐ _____
  _____
  _____

☐ _____
  _____
  _____

How can we resolve the issues we can't compromise on without creating any resentment?

☐ _____
_____

☐ _____
_____

If you can't agree on the things you can't compromise on, have an honest in depth conversation about them, create a pros and cons list for each thing, then revisit the issue again in a few months to see if anything has changed.

Pros : | **Cons :**

What is my idea of "the perfect date?"

☐ _____
   _____

   _____

☐ _____
   _____

   _____

What do I feel that we could do more of within our relationship?

☐ _____
   _____

   _____

☐ _____
   _____

   _____

What do I feel that we could do less of within our relationship?

☐ _____
   _____

   _____

☐ _____
   _____

   _____

What are some of my favorite things that you do for me?

☐ _____
   _____
   _____

☐ _____
   _____
   _____

Dates I would like us to go on in the near future:

☐ _____
   _____
   _____

☐ _____
   _____
   _____

List 3 ways we can begin loving one another better starting this week!

☐   ☐

A word from Stace:

Learning how to love one another properly can improve your relationship tenfold! While I was showering Josh with hugs and kisses and writing him love notes, he just wanted to be motivated and inspired. While he was motivating me and pushing me to be focused, I just wanted to be held! That's not to say that we didn't appreciate one another for what we were already doing, we were just hoping to have our love languages incorporated as well. Since we've spoken about it, our relationship could not seem more perfect & its all thanks to communication & a better understanding of how the other person wants to be loved!

Section Recap: How do I feel?

What did you learn about loving one another better?

☐ _____
_____
_____
_____

☐ _____
_____
_____
_____

Cater-to-you Date!

Yay! You're almost at the end of your "Just you & I" journey! For this last date you will take what you learned as well as what you already know to cater to your partner for an entire day. This means you will need to decicate two days, one for each of you, to conduct the most epic dates ever for each other!

What you should keep in mind:

- Your boo's favorite food spots

- Take a look at the previous list you both made under the "**Dates I would like us to go on in the near future**" question!

- Consider and incorporate the way bae likes to be loved:
  - **Experiences**
  - **Cuddles**
  - **Presents**
  - **Quality time together**
  - **Do some chores**
  - **Cook a meal & more**

- Put your heart in it, make one another feel loved in any way that you can!

- Enjoy, have fun, & take lots of pics! (& don't forget to hashtag #justyouandibook)

Section 7

Weekly Meetings!

Section 7: Weekly Meetings

I didn't know how necessary weekly relationship meetings were until I noticed how much can happen within a week. At first, when we decided to do meetings, we were doing them on a monthly basis. That lasted about 3 months until we decided that too much was happening to track over such a long period of time; instead, we came up with weekly meetings! So what the heck is a weekly meeting anyway and why did we start doing them? Well, Josh and I are all about self care and growth and they both are literally all about preventing horrible things like burnout or pressure buildup from occuring! We love each other and want our relationship to withstand the test of time, so just like our health, our businesses, and our mental states, we started to keep track of our relationship as well! The topics of our meetings change weekly; if we had a great week, we'll simply ask about how the week went, how we can have an even better week next week and so on and so forth. If we had a bad day during the week or even an entirely bad week, we'll use our meeting to dig deep to see what the root cause of our problems were and then we'll figure out what we can change so that next week will be better. The concept is simple, I'll explain our template in detail in the coming pages!

In this section, you will:

- Understand the breakdown of a weekly meeting
- Review the template and create one of your own for your weekly check-ins!

Our Weekly Meeting Template!

Use the template below to create your own weekly meetings! Feel free to modify questions as you see fit! Remember, the purpose of these meetings are to promote conversation, so don't worry about what you're going to write down, only write down your key points when you're ready to move on to the next question! **I have a special journal available only on Amazon for those who would like to support me, titled, "Our Journal", but feel free to use a notebook instead!**

Today's date: _/_/_ *This is for when you look back in a few months to see how much progress you've made!*

Mood starting our meeting:
   Name of Partner 1: *(rating from 1-10 + emotion)*
   Name of Partner 2: *(rating from 1-10 + emotion)*
   Be specific with your emotion (sad, happy, angry, frustrated, etc.)

List 3 positive things about your partner:
This starts the meeting off on a positive note even if you've had a bad week or day (positive things can be anything from kind things they did for you throughout the week, to characteristics you just like about your partner in general)

Give a brief overview of how you felt your week went:
Here's where you will go over the week to highlight the amazing things that happened or the not so great things that may need some revisiting. Talk about everything
especially the things that may need closure.

Did we have any miscommunications or disagreements this week?
Be honest with the disagreements that you had this week and hold yourselves accountable for your role in them.

How can we resolve any of the issues we had this week?
Come up with solutions that are realistic and can be implemented right away. There's nothing worse than an unresolved issue that later turns into resentment.

What are some of the things we spoke about working on last week? Did we fix those issues? If not, what efforts have been made to fix what we spoke about?
Here is your chance to revisit the issues you had last week to see if any of them have been resolved or are currently being worked on.

How can we ensure that we will have an amazing week (or another amazing week) next week?
Find ways to keep the happiness going. You won't have perfect weeks every week, but you can try your best to!

Outside of our relationship, how is everything going?
Talk about work, family, goals, happy moments, anything!

Ending notes or thoughts:
Briefly recap your meeting!

Mood ending the meeting:
    Name of Partner 1: *(rating from 1-10 + emotion)*
    Name of Partner 2: *(rating from 1-10 + emotion)*
    Ending your meeting with another mood-o-meter helps track if your meeting improved your mood!

Tip: Remember to have fun, it doesn't have to be 100% serious!

The End!

The End

Thank you for sticking with me 'til the end of this book. Again, your support means the world to me!

Here are some final tips for you before I let you go:

Love yourself first

Loving yourself first may sound like the biggest cliché out there, but it's true, if you genuinely love yourself, you will not allow anything negative into your life, simply because you will understand that you are worth more than that.

Put your pride to the side

Pride is another killer of relationships. Be mindful of when you are allowing your pride to get in the way.

Never stop growing

Everyday we have a new opportunity to learn and grow. Learn from everyone around you, even the most unsuspecting people have some gems to share with you.

Stay consistent with your meetings

I recommend that you stay very consistent with your meetings. Simply dedicating one hour a week to sitting down with your partner and discussing your goals can save you a lot of headaches in the future!

Sometimes you have to let go

Although this book promotes staying together and working through the obstacles, I highly recommend parting ways if the relationship seemingly has no hope or if you notice that your values aren't aligned.

Did you know?

If you support my friends over at *Bonding Bee's* you're supporting me as well!

How, might you ask?

By using my 10% discount code on any of their subscription box packages, *Bonding Bee's* will contribute a portion of your purchase to the progression of my book! What a sweet deal!

What is *Bonding Bee's* anyway?

Bonding Bee's is a monthly subscription box that supplies surprise dates each month to couples for them to enjoy from the comfort of their homes! That's right, you don't have to plan a thing or leave the house! Just sit back, relax, and wait for your next box to arrive to enjoy a unique date with your sweetheart each month!

Bonding Bee's also nominates "couples of the month" each month, the winning couple chooses a charity to donate to - a company with a purpose, what's not to love!?

So what are you waiting for? Head to:
www.BondingBees.com

My special 10% Promo Code:
JUSTYOUANDI

Consistency is the seed that sprouts success.

- Stacey Jailall

Follow Me on Social Media!

Instagram: @Stacey_Jayyy
Facebook: /staceymjayy
Twitter: @stacey_jayyyy

& Don't forget to use the hashtag
#Justyouandibook
on all of the amazing pictures you take
that are inspired by this book!

Thank you again for your support!
I appreciate you more than I could ever
put into words!

www.ingramcontent.com/pod-product-compliance
Lightning Source LLC
Chambersburg PA
CBHW041353290426
44108CB00006B/134